The Soul and Finding its Purpose on the Earth

By

Sara Khan

Contents:-

1. Dedication:-

I am dedicating the book to a brother that spiritually inspires me on the earth.

His inspiration words that are in my praise,

"A person who is a source of good, who instinctively helps others will always get distracted no matter how hard they try to remain focused. Just remember this, before you get distracted, by completing these books you will help so many more than you can imagine! So focus!"

May he silently continue to inspire me spiritually?

2. Introduction:-

There is a lot of hatred in the world where we live in today. If we want to see change, we ourselves need to be brave and change the way how we think. Nothing is going to improve until we learn to respect and value to each other. If you carry on showing hate, that is what the universe will give you back in return. Replace your negative thoughts into positive ones that our creator will be proud to hear from his creations and make them in a loving vibration.

This life is a test set before us from God and He is watching the actions that we, all are displaying. You could have those that show you hatred in the world today, but you must not do the same towards them and instead of shower those with loving thoughts from afar as you must bear in mind; the world isn't your final destination. Those that show hatred towards others, they will be tested themselves and it doesn't make it right if you show the same.

We, all think in our own way that we have some sort of power, but nothing in the world is more powerful than the thoughts that we send out, as that is our connection to our higher self. That higher self is surrounded by other souls that have lived before our time and they are besides us to guide ourselves on the earth. If we try, we can connect with them via vibration, that feeling and thoughts. Do try to connect to that deep thinking and you will feel a vibration of feelings that come in thoughts by our guides that our creator has assigned designated souls that have being blessed with so much wisdom that they will fill your head with so much beauty that will leave you wondering where those thoughts have come from, but have faith in what you get and use what you've being given wisely as we, all have thoughts and they can come in various forms.

Do be careful though, as our minds can also be very negative and at times disturbing. But if you feel this happening to you, it can be turned back into positive thoughts as you will find as you travel the journey of life that you are the one that's in charge of your body. The thoughts that you will get can sometimes come from your subconscious and you have to determine if they are what you want in your life. If you don't like what you get, you have the right to dismiss them by clearing your mind and telling your soul that it's your responsibility to control how you think as it's your body. At times we can get thoughts that can be so negative and if you do get these, try your hardest to turn them back into positive ones.

3. Self-Discovery:-

At some point in our lives, it will be a time in life where we will have many questions of what is the purpose of our existence on the earth. We would have searched in various places of the deep inner questions that niggle in our hearts of the whys but you would have looked and you might think that you hadn't got the answers yet to what you were searching for. But they will come in later life, as all the answers will eventually fit together like a jigsaw puzzle is coming together. Until that time comes, have patients with yourself and keep learning the many lessons that will come into your life as those obstacles, those lessons are part of your development for you to grow as a person.

Do bear in mind, even the strongest of people will face hardships in this life but just remember the difficulties that you face today are purely to test your strength in the *Duniya* (world) to prepare you for the next world. So do take the many tests that enter your life and do try your hardest to see them through. As these troubled times enter your life, you might think to yourself why me and you mustn't give up because of these hard times that come your way but you face the challenges ahead.

At times you will find which have so much in your mind, but no one to share them and this is the time that you can write your feelings onto a piece of paper to off load. Write down your thoughts on that paper, keep it or screw it up and put it in the bin. Don't ever keep the troubles you face inside to burden your soul, let it out and lighten your shoulders. As you do this exercise, you will feel the weight of your shoulders lighten and you will be free of that heavy burden that you've being carrying.

You will find that some will try their hardest to destroy that inner space, that wonderful place that you would have built for yourself with maliciousness directed towards you but try not to let it destroy what you have created for yourself. In your heart you will feel let down and hurt with someone else's negativity but try your hardest to not let this get you down, it's a test and part of life.

4. Finding "You":-

I didn't go looking for peace; I just looked at my life and put what was wrong right. I wouldn't say, it was easy but I took that big step and everything that I am is because of this step that I took and all the goodness that entered my life just flowed into place.

Tasks before you go to sleep tonight;

Before you go to sleep tonight, ask your soul a question, make it simple and only one as you don't want to confuse your soul. Then in the morning, you will get an answer and it will come in many ways. It can come in dreams, symbolically or any way our creator and your guides choose to give it to you. But you must write it down quickly because on awakening, you will most likely forget and the answer that has given to you will disappear from your mind. Do bear in mind that our souls are always wondering and it never sleeps. They spend hours searching for your answers from the spiritual world to help you on the earth and do try your best to have an open mind to receive what's being given to you.

If you're lucky to find out what you're purpose in life and the reason why you've being sent to the earth and what your role is in the life? You will feel relieved that after all that soul searching you finely to get to meet the newness of you. Finding you will come with challenges as not everyone will understand your new role, the new you and you will find that some people will leave you but be strong and let them go as their part in your life has come to the end. If you've found yourself on the path of discovery, you must keep moving forward and the answers that you search will be put in front of you but you must keep an open mind to find these hidden clues.

The answers could come in thoughts or visions and you must pay attention to what comes before you.

5. Say Goodbye:-

Everyone is not meant to walk on the path alongside to you and you must build a strong stomach and let them go. At first it will be hard, but in time, the cravenness that you feel will lesson in time, the urge to see them will go as you would have met new people that would have entered into your life. Everyone is in your life to deliver a lesson and when they have done that, let them go as they've done their bit on your path. As you see some people in your life disappearing, God will be clearing the path to let new people in and they have already being destined to be part of your journey, that path you walk. So don't be too shocked when you let one or two go and see the exact amount enter your life in return. At first when you see this materialising, you will be amazed that it's happening right in front of your eyes but don't be too dazed as that is how the sequence of the universe operates. We are only on the earth living a test and the real experience will start in the afterlife which you have to earn your place in. It will hurt when you let those that cause you mischief go and this emptiness that you feel will eventually pass.

6. The Afterlife:-

We have at times all wondered what the afterlife could be like or had grown up with the idea that the heaven is high in the sky and out of our reach. Most of us would have wondered where the place that we call heaven could be. But that heaven isn't very far as you might have imagined it to be, it's very close and it's within you, that energy, that love that surrounds you is your heaven and you yourself are that heaven. As heaven is within you, you must always try your best to make your body a loving place as that is where God resides too and you wouldn't want him to be in your space if you have thoughts that aren't in a loving nature? Even if you do have concerns in your life, He won't leave you but help you and try his hardest to get you onto the next step of your growth as he knows problems are only temporary but don't leave it up to him to do all the work for you, you must also work at the issues that you are facing. As we get older, we can at times be frightened of death, it can be a scary thought but you will learn to love that fear that comes with it, as passing over is just going into another dimension. That place is an opening of two worlds that will open up when your soul is ready to depart the world on the earth and a loved one will come to collect your soul for your new spiritual journey that will consist of no pain.

7. My Visualisation of the Heaven: That Final Resting Place:-

In my imagination, I have the picture that paradise is a beautiful place and out of the world. It consists of bright blue skies, green grass that will be so soft to touch and flowers of all varieties. We will have houses with all floors, containing kitchen, living area and bedrooms. When you open the bedroom window, the view will be of the countryside and the sun will shine onto your face. The breeze will touch your skin, that sensation of calmness and peace all around you. There will be other souls and not necessarily your beloved ones that are on the earth now. There will be loved ones and other souls from other lives that have being travelling on your journey spiritually. We won't be communicating by voice, it will be via thoughts and there will be no bitterness, only lovely echoes. You will hear birds humming, colourful butterflies and swans, floating in the lake. There will be smells of fragrances, sweet perfume and essential oils. There will still be schools as you will still continue to grow and you will be taught by the guides that have wisdom from the higher guides that have being there hundreds of years. We won't have our bodies; just our souls and we will float everywhere. You will have that feeling of touch and there will be all sorts of fruits but you won't eat them physically but you will taste them via your imagination. There will be all sorts of levels and on each layer of the heaven there will be different kinds of souls. All souls will have to earn their place to reach each level, like a test. When you first cross over, there will be white light that you will go through. First level will be like a hospital for lost souls who are confused and scared of what has just happened to them, that death. Some will bypass this level as they have already grown spiritually on the earth and have earned their place in the paradise, a place of beauty, a place of pure peace.

The top level will be the highest of the highest and that will be where our creator will be, waiting for his creation to return back home and to look at your life. The hell will be beside a glass and the souls that are residing there will only look at this beauty and will take thousands of years to earn their place in the paradise.

This is my views on what the paradise will look like and only time will tell when it's my turn to return back home.

8. Our Guide from Spiritual World:-

When our soul is sent to the earth in the body of a new born baby, we don't come alone as we are accompanied by a guide from the spiritual world that will stay with us on the time that we are on the earth. This guide will not leave us and at times we will have various other guides that will enter into our life but they will only be at our side for short periods of the lesson that we might need at that precise time of our life. Not everyone will now of this but we can learn to talk to them and they will in return send messages back in thoughts. This is where you will need to be very alert and careful with what thoughts you pick up on and some won't even get this connection as the universe might feel that you're not ready to receive guidance at this time of your life, as many lessons still would need to be learned yet. Keep learning by every teaching that enters into your life, as you're experiencing the many lessons, they won't make sense at that time but when your time is right all these lessons will all slot into place, like a jigsaw puzzle coming together. As you reach at this stage, your guide might appear and start to guide you in life and in time, you will feel the messages that they will be sending your way.

9. Communicating to your other Half's Soul:-

Marriages are made in the heaven and to experience on the earth but I know it can be hard at times. I'm going to share one of my secrets to a successful marriage that you can all do by talking to your other half's soul. All our energy is in the physical body that have come to the earth to experience life. Our creator does pair us up before our birth, with that he attaches our destiny and gives us choices.

You can all talk to your other half's soul as we are all energy in a shell that we call a body. But before you start to communicate, you must ask for permission as around our bodies we are protected by door keepers, and not only that, we have a primary guide who has being with us from the moment when we are born. You ask for permission in your mind and you will know if you have got it by the feelings that you will experience. A loving tingling feeling is a 'yes' and if you feel weird then it's a big 'no'. Their soul will block you and you mustn't continue with this exercise.

When you have got the connection, start your conversation and just tell them how your feeling. Just off load all your problems that are in your mind. It's just like having a conversation if they were next to you and then, watch during the weeks as you see changes occurring.

The next step….

You can actually give instructions to each other's souls via your minds and tell them what you want or desire and if you're both spiritually connected you will both pick up on each other's thoughts.

10. My Hubby Saw My Soul as He Rushed to Save Someone's Life:-

My hubby had to rush someone to hospital as they had a reaction to a nut allergy. As he was driving like mad to get this person to hospital on his right shoulder he saw my soul spiritually standing beside him. I was dressed in a brown sari with red lipstick, smiling and giving him comfort. He said that I stayed with him until he got to the hospital. He felt that I was guiding him to get them there safely as he drove through red lights. At the same time, I do remember and I phoned him to say that I was feeling so tired. This explained why I was feeling tired as my energy was being used spiritually elsewhere. Our souls do travel while we are sleeping and when we are awake doing our daily chores. This person could have died that day if it wasn't for my husband and me. As he was telling me that I could see his face, that shock of disbelieve as to what had just happened and I had spirit with me at the same time, that beautiful fragrance that they normally sprinkle all around my surroundings.

11. Conclusion:-

Our souls have come here to learn lessons from the
earthly ways and to take back what they've learned back
to a higher place in the afterlife. All our souls are trying
to earn their place in the many layers of the heaven and
most that know of this is trying their best to reach the top
layer in our creators' house and to spend eternity with
him. There will be some that won't be able to achieve it,
as they will fail on the many tests that will be put in front
of them but they shouldn't let this dishearten them as you
can still continue to grow in the afterlife. Just because
your life on the earth has ended, your soul will always
continue living and continue aiming for the place that is
filled with tranquillity of pure beauty.

So walk your path and go which ever direction your heart
takes you but God will always be there waiting on your
return. He will let you search for yourself and experience
what is out there in the world that he created for you. You
will fall many times and you will feel his hands of
support as you try to find your way. You will question
everything that comes in your way, turn every stone
upside down but that is your strength being built as you
walk your path. That strength will help you in the future
when you have come close to him. On your final
destination, the place that was created for you will be full
of love and that strength which you built on your travels
will help you on the last bit of your journey. Others will
try their utmost best to knock you back down and back to
their reality as they will not recognize the place that you
are at. But don't you worry as there was a purpose for all
those tears and pain that you went through. As you were
shredding those tears, he was collecting them on your
behalf. As you were struggling in life, he was there
walking in your footsteps so that when you fell, he could

catch you. On many occasions, he would have caught you and you would have felt that warm air all around you, the feathers that he scattered all around you. You must have felt them as you fell to the ground but you got straight back up, didn't you. Know that you have seen what is out there, in the world that he created for you. It's time for you to use all your experiences and guide others onto the path of pure peace. The struggle that you experienced will be their strength now but you show the world that it's ok to stumble, get lost as the final destinations into the paradise, which has being already written. But remember that you will have support from your brothers and sisters who will help you to guide others onto the right path that you are travelling on. So never worry of the many questions that will be asked of you as he will send support your way to guide and help you. They will try their best to knock you back down but it will be your challenges as you search the answers to their questions which will be asked of you. You just carry on and deliver his message of pure peace and don't be afraid as on your last breath, he will send thousands of angels to come and collect you. He knows that you have already felt this presence as it was a taster to show you what it is like to feel angels carrying you. Picture that journey whose you went on, but only this time you will not be returning back to the earth like the last time. They will carry you gently into the heaven and on your return your life will be played back. Yes, every thought, every action that you took would have being registered and he will talk you through your life.

12. The Words from My Soul

In the life, in your troubles, you will find that your shadow will never leave you and it will always be one step ahead or besides you. The people who come into your life, be it for love or to do mischief are the lessons of life. You keep going and if there is darkness shadowing in your life, it will disappear as you take them the magical steps of life. Just keep going and take those challenges that have come your way. No one knows you better than yourself, so have faith and don't let doubt get in the way.

On your travels in the life, you will get lost, misguided and came across so many crossroads. At the end of each road, you will stop and think, is this the right way? You will sometimes take the wrong road, but it won't be all bad as it will be lessons for the future. When you finely reach that right path, you will know as it will feel right. But as you walk on your journey that your creator wrote in your destiny, you will get others who will think that you're on the wrong path. But you listen to that gut, that deep feeling as that will be the God communicating and directing you to the light. You keep going and you will get so many knock backs but you get back up. You will do this, as on your travels the God will carry you, like he did when you was oppressed, he will never leave you alone. You just take them steps and trust in what you are given. Your inner faith will get you to your destination and your hearts desires will become a reality. So it's ok to take the wrong path, as it's all lessons of life. Believe in what you have being given and take the step if it feels right. Once you start walking on the right path, there is no going back and it's all full of joy.
Justice, doesn't always mean that?

As you go through the life and finely see the end in sight. It is emotional looking back at what once was and how far you have come. What a journey? I have had and look at what is waiting for me at the top of this amazing ladder of the life. My message as always, if something needs fixing, it's your job, your life, your responsibility and you're in charge. So stand up and take back what was already yours and take control. There will still be times when you fall back down. Be strong and stand up and fight. There is a lot of support out there. Strangers who you would never have met will reach out their hand. Hold that hand tight and never let go. Have faith in yourself as you are strong. Be that person that you attended to be. I will be there giving you strength and if not in person but spiritually.

If you listen to your inner feelings you too will get the answers within. Dig deep into your soul and there will be the answer that you search.

In life there will be many lessons send your way, and there will always be reasons as to why and more teaching, learning and to progress further. But never blame the person delivering the message, as the lesson had to be learned. But the question is, what did you learn from the experience? The world is full of corruption and hatred. Now, as I face it on a regular basis. Why people can't love and just get on, I will never now but that's their choice, their destiny that they chose to live on the earth. Yes, I'm different and now, I don't fit in, but this is how my destiny was written. Yes, I've put up a fight to become the person that I am today but I am proud to be me.

Just thinking back, turned all that hate in my life into the pure love. How did I do that? That's a good question.

To find this divine within you, is so powerful and I do urge you to find it too but it does come with a price. Yes, left the whole lot of them but you might think that's selfish. It's not; they were lessons of life and just played a part in your life.

Remember all the answers that we search within us. Just needs you to dig deep and search.

You might be going through a hard time as you progress in life but never forget that you are important. The barriers of steal will get broken but always tread your path with respect, dignity and honesty. If others raise their voice, you stay quiet. Do not rise to them as they are not on your level and do not understand what you feel. Always eat and look after you as you need to be strong to continue with the task laid in front of you. Travel your path with love and peace in mind. One day they will understand what you are doing and will come around. I am always going to continue with my journey which my soul has desired.

So go and get your hearts desires but walk your path with respect and dignity in mind.

We, all have a journey in life, starting from that first breath to those steps onwards. We, all have stories, and you never will get to the ending as life will never end. Along the way, you take them steps and they could be magical if you let them be or they could be filled with pain. The choice will always be yours as the God gave us free will and we have a duty to ourselves to live an honest life. I said, life never ends, even on your last breath; your life will be played back to you. Now, you choose what you wish to see, be it good or be it bad but the choice will be yours. If you want to be led away by angels and be surrounded by magical light, take them magical steps of life.

Life is good and is going to get even better, this transformation, this amazing change is accepted with love. We are purely energy within a body that have come to experience life on the motherland, the earth. If you want your life to be this good, take back control. It's your life, your responsibility and you're in charge. It could take a day, month or years but you do get there. There will be so many obstacles and stones thrown at your direction but keep going and don't stop. You will get there as I will be holding your hand to guide you. That is my word to you and most of you, all I keep my promises, now. Life is on the track and going in the right direction. I ask and the universe delivers, we have a good partnership.

We should learn by each lesson sent our way, if it comes again, that lesson isn't learned or I need to really stop craving what will never be. But my heart must be getting stronger with the time, as I had a fantastic sleep. Always look at what is in front of you; I'm looking at my two boys fighting over what to watch on TV. This is how my destiny was written; The God took all my blood family away from me, as they had taught me the lessons that I had to take from them. But he made sure; I had a family that I made to replace them all. My rock, that's my husband who is my support and he will always stand next to me on this wonderful journey. My little boys, yes, they drive me mad but they are my world and I will protect them forever. Then I have two sisters in law who are more as sisters and they are the sisters that I had lost. Then you are my world who is my strength and in time my love for you, all has grown so big.

"Yesterday I learned, a daughter is for lifetime and not only for a short time. I'm sure that you, all will happily accept this daughter by heart and then I can stop craving what will never happen, as it wasn't written in my destiny to receive love from my blood family".

As I drove to work it was so dark and there are people in the world who have this darkness in themselves. I once had it too much and it's very hard to get that light in place. But if you keep searching, you will find that bright light and then, there are people who like the darkness in their lives.

Dreams are meant to be explored and lived; you dream it and the world will deliver. You will take some steps back and think, is this for the real, I am really doing this. Yes, you are, so continue with bringing that dream alive. My dream has a magic message for the world to gain their inner peace. They will look and the feelings that I get, they will feel too with all their heart. I will be their voice that is so faint. I will raise my voice and send out this message of peace. I believe in me and you will too. All this happiness and peace aren't for me to keep locked in. It has to be shared and with respect. I feel that I am the daughter, sister that someone else let go of but the world opened their arms and accepted me for the person that I truly am. For this honour I will pass the message of pure peace into the lives of many. I am their daughter and I will deliver this message. My life, my peace belongs to the world as I will give it all away, that is my word and I always work with honesty.
Remember each thought that you have. That thought will become your reality so make it good. I will show you how to do that. Just ask me as I know that you will.
Peace is on its way. Just believe.

All this happiness and peace aren't for me to keep locked in, It has to be shared and with the respect. I feel that I am the daughter, sister that someone else let go of but the world opened their arms and accepted me for the person that I truly am. For this honour I will pass the message of peace into the lives of many. I am their daughter now and I will deliver my message. My life, my peace belongs to the world as I will give it all away. This is my word to you all and I always work with honesty. Remember each thought that you have, will become your reality so make it good. I will show you how to do that. Just ask me as I know that you will. If you have a desire to dream, to make your name and to be successful, then do it, be brave and go for it. You will make mistakes along the way but you will learn from those experiences. My heart's desire is to have my name worldwide and I believe that I will accomplish my goal. I believe in me as I am very important and loved by me. As I am reaching at my goals, I will help souls that I meet on my travels. I will guide you and teach you what I have learned in my journey. That is my promise to the world and I have helped so many souls already.

As your inner strength gets stronger as you develop there will be others who will not be able to keep up with your pace. Be strong and continue on your path even if it means leaving them to hide. If you choose to change your destination you will not be able to complete the path that you came to accomplish in this lifetime. Be strong and continue to be you as you are loved by millions.

Paths that will lead you into God's arms

In life there will be many paths that will lead you into God's arms. Be it peace, love and faith but you will do it in your way and in your own time. We come to the earth to learn lessons and experience human race. Whatever comes into your way will be valuable lessons sent your way. Don't argue with the messenger but take note and say thank you. There will be so much learning to do and you will progress slowly by all the teaching sent your way. Lots of new souls will come into your life and you will think for a second, is this for the real; yes, it is. It was already planned in your destiny before you came onto the earth. These souls were meant to come into your life and to help you on your journey that you have found yourself on. Whatever comes your way will always be valuable lessons sent to teach you about life. It's ok to look at as many materials as possible to gain knowledge.

Life doesn't always stay the same

Life doesn't always stay the same as with time and taking
those amazing steps it does to get better. What do you go
through in life are lessons that you came to explore on the
earth to experience. This was what was written in your
destiny and then there is that word "free will" that others
cross your path to suit their needs or choices. This was
the God's choice to attach that to your lives. But with
hard work and determination you can get back onto your
intended paths and complete this journey that you came
to learn from. We are all on different stages in life and
you have a duty to yourselves to complete this journey.
There will be obstacles that come your way but you must
be strong and deal with them. Nothing in life is simple
and if you listen very carefully to your inner thoughts
there are the answers of your questions which you want
to find. When you do get the answer that you have been
searching for, be brave and act on the information being
given.

Determination

Never give up as you do get to see the ending of your life story. What a life I have had and look what's waiting at the end of this amazing journey. Never hold your tears in as everyone that you shred has a value attached to it. I really have cried all my life and I was meant to so that I could heal the world and that's you all.

Believe in Yourself

To get to this point in the life only you, you self can get there. Believe in yourself and you will get to your destination. There will be angels who will come onto your path. Accept them, as they have being sent by God and already written in your destiny. We can all get to this point but you have to take the first step.

Energies in a Physical Body

We are all energies in a physical body with powerful thoughts that can change you as the person. When we have grown and become this wonderful energy, it's our duty to pass all the knowledge that you have learned to the world so that they too can start their journey. Keep sending your thoughts of wisdom and peace will start to grow. It is infectious and addictive so please keep going. What we do now will matter as we will leave a legacy for the future children that are to come into the world.

Life does get better and you do find that peace within.

From now on the life will just keep getting better and better. Everyone can get to this stage but it takes some tough steps that you need to climb. Be strong, take these amazing steps and watch as your life shines as it will just keep sparkling. Have faith in the most wonderful person in the world and that is "you" believe as you do it. Put all your heart into gaining this gift that you have earned. The last lot of tears are the hardest of all but you will come past them. It's all part of your journey that you came to experience in this life. You will leave people in your life behind you but from where lessons that came onto your path to teach you the values of life. Be it bad or good; deal with it and then move onto the next step. Your future is in your hands, as it's your life. Yes, remember that the word "your life" there will be others who will try to stop you but take their advice, listen and don't raise your voice. In time they will too understand that this is your path which you have to travel. Do thank them for finely understanding though. That's one thing that I haven't done yet. Yes, need to thank my closest and dearest for letting me travel my path in peace.

Spread Love and Peace

Today, my message is spread love and peace to whomever you might meet on your travels. Send loving thoughts to the people that have hurt you in the past. Without them lessons you wouldn't be the person that you are today. This might sound harsh but hate will destroy you and the people who did wrong will be the winners. You become that winner; show them and the world that you have survived. All the goodness that you have put in this year you will be rewarded. You either step onto the ladder of this amazing change or stay where you are? The decision is in your hands.

Always love yourself first and you will get angels sent your way. Just met the most amazing person that you could ever meet, you could see it in her eyes the love she had for this stranger. I'm not that stranger anymore as I will be there for her to hold her hand for however long she needs me. I will be her guide on the earth and do my best to support her. Then I was also blessed with another angel that was with her. I could feel the tears from this other angel. I do feel blessed that the God is sending me lovely souls my way. I will be there for anyone who needs me and that is a promise.

We are all energies in a physical body with powerful thoughts that can change you as a person. When we have grown and become this wonderful energy, it's our duty to pass all the knowledge that you have learned to the world so that they too can start their journey. Keep sending your thoughts of wisdom and peace will start to grow. It is infectious and addictive so please keep going. What we do now will matter as we will leave a legacy for the future children that are to come into the world.

In life there will be many obstacles that come knocking at your door. But you stop; you think are these right, am I doing the right thing and am I meant to be here. Then you listen to that gut, that feeling and that voice within. You feel that sensation, you trust and then you act. Yes, that word, trust is a very powerful tool and you believe in what you have being given.

I never believed in 'hope' as I'm a person who does it. If you hope, you're not really serious about your niche. Well I was wrong, as there is hope and my beloved God, Allah and the spiritual world are looking after me as I take this vocation that I am on. I do have angels who are holding my hand as I travel this amazing journey in this life time. They were there for me once again, with that strong hand of support. So yes, believe within you but don't lose that hope. Every step of the way, you will be taken care of. So never stop asking them questions, and the answers will come. Even the answer came in the words of hope. That's my next step, and I'm taking this journey slowly.

Ask and you will receive but do it with a clean heart. If your soul is pure, it will work that magic on your behalf. If you're not ready, work on your steps and make changes in your life. Then listen to your gut, that feeling as that is your inner soul sending you messages. Be brave and act on that feeling as that is your future. Life will not change overnight but it will with time. Don't give up on the first try, keep going and motivate yourself. You have come to the earth with a mission, so dig deep into your soul as all the answers are already within.

In life there will be many lessons sent your way, and there will always be reasons as to why, more teaching, learning and to progress further. But never blame the person delivering this message, as the lesson had to be learned. But the question is, what did you learn from the experience? The world is full of corruption and hatred. Why people can't love and just get on, I will never know but that's their choice, their destiny that was chosen for them to live on the earth. Yes, I'm different and I know I don't fit in, but this is how my destiny was written. Yes, I've put up a fight to become the person that I am today but I am proud to be me.

To find this divine within is so powerful and I do urge you to find it too but it does come with a price. Remember all the answers that we search our already within, just needs you to dig deep and search. Luckily I believe in forgiveness, as hatred and hurtfulness doesn't get you anywhere in life. Forgive and move on. Done it before and I will do it again. Just remember, every action that you take, think, how it is going to affect the recipient and it is always a good idea to discuss, before doing it. Yes, I have being gifted with this divine powerful gift, and I mustn't waste it on pettiness. I have a responsibility to deliver these spiritual messages that I receive from Guides before my time and I will do it with respect and dignity in mind.

Reach deep down and you too will find that hidden faint voice. Go deeper, as it is there, all lost, alone and waiting to get louder. When it does finely get raised, don't put it back where you found it from. Keep on using it and you will be surprised at the rewards that will be gifted to you. They might not come in money, but in bundles of love and smiles. Treasure that voice, as it's returned to the rightful owner and it belongs to you. You are the owner of this great gift that was well hidden and lost to the world. Now the world will hear this voice, so do make it clear and with conviction. The feelings that you will get with this gift are just magical and will be treasured for life.

As we take each step in our daily lives, there will be lots levels that you will come across. There will be steps that you will step on easily, or climb onto and you could miss a step. But whatever stage you might be at, tread very carefully. Do not hate, or send out negative thoughts, even to your enemies as they are purely here to teach you a lesson in order for you to get onto the next step. Lessons of life will never stop coming and there will always be new lessons as you leave behind previously. Then there will be people that you leave behind as they have done their work and taught you the lessons that you needed to learn. Don't go back, move forward and enjoy life. On your travels of life, you will get many opportunities put before you. But the choice will be yours, do you take that step or walk on by, again. Find the strength within to come out your comfort zone and take that chance as it will get easier as you progress in life.

As your confidence grows, don't forget to look back at others who might need help. When you have established yourself and are very confident, there will be others who will look at what you do and just keep looking. What I say to them is be brave and join in. We all started from the bottom and we were like you once. You have to push yourself and just get out there and do whatever your heart desires. You too can get to the top, but only you can make that happen. You will be surprised how many will hold out their hand and hold your hand tight.

Be brave and step onto the ladder of success. We confident people will stop and answer your questions. So don't be afraid to ask that question or two that you have.

Confidence does not just happen. You have to work at it and build them layers. It's up to you how you progress but if someone offers their support be brave and accepts. We all started from the bottom and built them layers.

Live a life of truth, clean heart and divine will enter your soul. If you find that there is something that needs sorting, take steps, be brave and that heart will heal. When you reach that state of pure happiness, well you are nearly there. Hold onto your breath, be very careful not to trip as greed will be sent your way and you will have to start all over again. Always live a peaceful life and follow your heart that gut as that's where our creator directs us in life.

In life, the God will set out your path and all he asks is for you to have trust in what he gives you, have faith and then be brave to walk that path that has being laid out for you.

As you go through life, learn the ways of the world and what the word destiny actually means. You will come to a point, that understanding, life is already planned and nothing is an accident. Everyone we meet, you were meant to as it was written like this by our creator. The path ahead is already planned and you just need to listen to your gut, that feeling and have strength to walk it! We have purely come to the earth to learn the ways of the world and will be taking all these teachings back home, to our creator. So get as much knowledge as you possibly can, the more you learn, the more you will progress and the higher you will reach on your final destination. There are still steps to climb in the afterlife when you take your last breath on the earth. Only a handful will get to the top of this step, that step is the purist of all and no one will now if you will or not. Just keep on the right path and don't let greed win.

In life there will be lots of mountains to climb, hard work involved and with persistence you will see the success. There will be knock backs but keep going and don't stop. At the end of this dark tunnel there will be light. When you see that light you have succeeded but don't forget the people you left behind. As one day they too will need guidance in their life again. They will need someone to help them where they have got lost. For now they can't see what is the right and the wrong but one day the time will come when they too will have to better themselves to make their life complete. God is watching every move that they are making and making notes.

Keep that faith and trust in you.

Only you will now when the time is the right to begin the journey of pure peace. When you do begin your journey, keep going and don't stop. There will be challenges sent your way; you take them as they will be tests. Tests to see how strong you can hold on, be strong and keep going as the end will be nearer. And on every corner, there will be an angel waiting to hold your hand. So never worry, stress or panic as it will all come together as that is how your destiny was written! Just get ready for the success and gifts that will come your way. Do enjoy, but never forget the people that held your hand do go back and help the next soul!

Look deep into your heart, go deeper and take a big breath. As you take each breath you will go deeper and there you will find your soul. When you get to that point clear your head with all the daily thoughts that you carry around with you. Keep taking them breaths and then relax! You will be ready to begin this journey of discovery of you! Remember mind blank and no thoughts. Listen to the quietness all around you. You might hear shuffles and you could feel a breeze touch your face. The most important of all, your soul will give you a message. It might come in thoughts, pictures or symbolically! Just relax and be you! Stay there for a few minutes and then slowly make your way back. Keep taking them deep breaths as you say good bye to your soul. Don't forget to thank them for their time. With each breath you take you will come back to the surface. Open your eyes and just relax.

Don't forget to share your experiences. Also to write it down as you will forget in a flash.

13. Thanking You

I would like to say thank you to all my followers, as your warm blessings and your support has moulded me into the person that I have become today. I truly love you all from the bottom of my heart and we may encourage each other to climb on each step of the life as it enters our lives. May God shower you all with his magical healing sprinkles and forever give you abundance in life!

"The soul is one of the things, of which the knowledge is only with my Lord. And of knowledge, you (Mankind) have been given only a little."] (Al-Israa' 17:85)

All my words that I write are yours to keep. Read them by your heart and let your healing begin. They are a gift from the God and wisdom from others before my time. I do feel blessed as the spiritual world never stops showing me how much they love me. I had some more amazing spiritual experiences last night. I did feel light as all the worries that I collect from your shoulders during the day were taken away. Every souls heart I touch you will forever be in my heart until my dying days. My words are yours; they belong to the world for you to begin your journey of pure love. I, for one, will never let go of your hand once I have caught you in my arms. I will never leave anyone behind as what I have learned isn't for me to keep lock up inside. I am always going to be here for others. That's my role in the life as I do work for the God and I am his creation. But you must help you too as your life is your responsibility. A good friend reminded me that my book isn't for me to keep, it belongs to the world and that is so true. It's good when friends give you good honest answers from the heart. This is my gift to the world so you too can start your journey of pure love and peace, believe me it can be done – I am living proof of that. You will know when the time is the right to begin your journey. My life did get better and I have found my inner peace within. This is my story. My hope is that in some way, it helps others on a journey of pure love.

Sara Khan

The Soul and its Purpose on Earth.

Made in the USA
Monee, IL
07 July 2026